The Ancestry of John R Stone of Spokane, WA

The Royal Lineage

By John and Patricia Stone

The Royal Lineage

Table of Contents

Forward

We owe our very existence to our ancestors. We would not be here except for our mothers and fathers. And they would not be here except for their parents. Our genetic makeup traces not only from them, but to all our ancestors back to the beginning of mankind. We cannot trace the line back to the beginning since that was before documented history and in most cases we can only go back a few hundred years. Our grandparents and great grandparents are usually as far back as our own memory and family photos will take us. After 1850 the Federal Census reports provide a wealth of information about US families and individuals. Before that the Census only listed head of household and numbers of people in age categories in the house. Unless your ancestor was a person of prominence or in the military the information will probably end at this generation. If we are lucky enough to find information as far back as the pilgrims in the 1600's, that is usually the end of the story since it is hard to trace these families into Europe. But in the happy event there is royalty in the line, the lineage can be traced back to the middle ages and even earlier since these stories are well known and many books have been written. The spelling of names varies since the records are transcribed from ancient languages.

By tracing the lineage of the female members of the John Stone family for many generations, we come to the name of Robert Stewart, an immigrant prisoner from Scotland, arriving in America in 1652 and first documented in Milford, Connecticut. Robert was not a common criminal but was a

The Royal Lineage

prisoner of war in a battle between Scotland and England and these prisoners were sent to America as slave labor in that year. Looking closely at the ancestry of Robert Stewart takes us back in time through the well documented House of Steward and we find many ancestors of royal descent, back to Robert the Bruce of Scotland and many of the Viking Kings of Sweden. We can go back in time long long ago to the middle ages, the time of knights and crusades and castles and royal intrigue, here is how the story goes:

Part I Robert the Bruce

Robert de Brus 1078 to 1141

Born in 1078, Robert de Brus I, also known as the 1st Lord of Annandale, was the founder of the Bruce dynasty. His parents were thought to be Adam de Brus and Emma de Ramsey. He was a Norman baron and knight. He came to England after King Henry I conquered Normandy. King Henry granted him many estates for his help in the battle. In 1124, After King Henry I died and King David I of Scotland took power, Robert was given the title of Lord of Annandale. When King Henry of England died, his successor was King Steven. King David of Scotland refused to recognize the new King of England, but Robert did support him, creating a rift in their friendship. Robert and his oldest son, Adam, joined the English army. Robert's younger son, Robert, jointed the Scottish forces in support of King David. He died in 1141, at the age of 63. His oldest son, Adam died a year later. His younger son, **Robert**, assumed the title of Annandale and carried on the family dynasty.

Figure 1 Robert de Brus Knight

Robert de Brus 1138 to 1194

Robert de Brus, 2nd Lord of Annandale, was born in 1138, when his father was 60 years old. Like his father, he was a Norman noble. He stayed loyal to King David I of Scotland and took over his father's lands in Scotland. He married Euphemia, daughter of the Count of Aumale. They had five known children, Robert, William, Bernard, Agatha and Euphemia. The eldest son Robert died before his father and second son **William** carried on the inheritance. Robert died in 1194, at the age of 56. He is buried at Gisborough Priory, a monastery founded by his father, located in North Riding, Yorkshire, England.

Figure 2 Gisborough Priory

William de Brus c1158 to 1212

William's birth date is unknown. He was the second son of
Robert, 2nd Lord of Annandale and became the 3rd Lord of
Annandale and inherited large estates in the north of England.
He married Beatrice de Teyden and they had at least two
sons, **Robert** and William. William died in July 16, 1212.

Robert de Brus 1195 to 1251

Born in 1195, Robert was the 4th Lord of Annandale. In about
1219 he married Isobel of Huntingdon (1199-1251), the great
granddaughter of King David I of Scotland. By this marriage
he acquired the manors of Writtle and Hatfield in Broadoak,
Essex, England. They had at least three children, Bernard,
Beatrice and **Robert**. Through this marriage the throne of
Scotland was established. He died in 1251, at the age of 56.

Robert de Brus 1220 to 1295

Carrying on the family heritage, he was the 5th Lord of
Annandale. In 1240 he married Lady Isabella de Clare (1226-
1264). They had 5 children, Isobel, **Robert**, William, Bernard
and Richard. After Isabella died he married Christina but they
had no children. He was a feudal lord, Justice and Constable
of Scotland and England, a Regent of Scotland and a

competitor for the Scottish throne in 1290-1292. He was known as Robert the Noble.

Figure 3 Robert "The Noble" de Brus

When Edward I of England was called on to decide which competitor should take the throne when the seven year old Queen died, he was unsuccessful but his family was still in line for the throne should the chosen king, John Balloil, die without an heir. King Edward I undermined the authority of King John and treated Scotland as a vassal state. This eventually led to the dethroning of John and the war for Independence. Robert died March 31, 1295 at Lochmaben Castle.

Figure 4 Lochmaben Castle under attack 1385

Robert de Brus 1243 to 1304

Robert was the 6th Lord of Annandale. He was born in July, 1243. In 1264, when he was only 18, he had to ransom his father who had been captured during the battle of Lewes. Legend has it that in 1270 he was participating in the 8th crusade when his friend Adam de Kilconquhar was killed. He took it upon himself to deliver the news to the widow, Marjorie. Marjorie was the Countess of Carrick living in Turnberry Castle. Marjorie immediately fell in love with the handsome Robert and held him captive in her castle until he agreed to marry her.

Figure 5 Turnberry Castle

In 1271 he married Marjorie, Countess of Carrick (1252-1292). Marjorie brought with her the title of Earl of Carrick for her son. As a knight, Robert served King Edward I of England and participated in the conquest of Wales. Robert brought a bloodline with a claim to the Scottish throne. He and Marjorie had eleven children before Marjorie died in 1292. The oldest son, **Robert**, was born in 1274. After the death of Marjorie he married Eleanor, but they had no children. He died in 1304 at the age of 61, on Easter, enroute to his estate in Annandale and is buried in Hol Cultrum Abbey

Robert the Bruce 1274 to 1329

Robert was born July 11, 1274. He was also known as King Robert I. He became King of Scotland in 1306 following the defeat of William Wallace at the Battle of Falkirk.. He was instrumental in defeating William Wallace as he sided with the

English and cut off the escape route of the Scottish forces. He became one of Scotland's greatest Kings.

Figure 6 Robert the Bruce

He led the wars of Independence and under his reign Scotland became an independent nation. He probably spent his early life fostered with a local family, as was the custom of the day. He would have spoken both French and Gaelic. As an heir to the throne, Robert would have been schooled by tutors and taught the requirements of courtly etiquette. He would have waited as a page at his father's and grandfather's tables. His grandfather, as an unsuccessful claimant to the throne, was a big influence on him. When King Edward I awarded the vacant throne of Scotland to a cousin, the Bruce's sided with King Edward against Scotland. His allegiance swung between Scotland and England but eventually he consolidated his power and was recognized as king of Scotland in 1309. The battle of Bannockburn in 1314 defeated England and asserted Scottish Independence.

Figure 7 Battle of Bannockburn led by Robert the Bruce

Before 1296 Robert married Isabella of Mar and they had one child, **Marjorie**, born in 1296. Isabelle died shortly after giving birth. In 1302 Robert married Elizabeth deBurgh. During the battles for independence King Edward was on the hunt for Robert. To keep them safe, he sent his wife, young daughter and sisters north to stay with his brother, Neil. Soon after,

The Royal Lineage

Neil's castle was captured and Neil was taken prisoner, later to be hanged, drawn and quartered. The ladies were also taken prisoner. Two of Robert's sisters were kept in iron cages and humiliated. Another was put in a nunnery. His wife was imprisoned in a castle and was treated better since her father was a friend of the King. His 12 year old daughter Marjorie was put in a nunnery. After the Battle of Bannockburn all the ladies were returned in a prisoner exchange. Robert and Elizabeth had four children, the last dying in infancy. He also had at least six illegitimate children by other mothers.

In 1327 Robert became ill with leprosy or some sort of neurological disorder. He undertook a journey in 1328 but was so ill he was carried in a litter all the way. In 1329 King Robert died at the age of 55. His body is buried in Dunfermline Abbey but his heart is buried in Melrose Abbey. His embalmed heart was taken on a crusade by his friend and lieutenant but only reached Granada where it was used as a talisman at the Battle of Teba.

Figure 8 Tomb of Robert the Bruce

Marjorie Bruce 1296 to 1316

Marjorie was the daughter of Robert the Bruce. At the time her father took the throne she would have been 10 years old. Her mother was Isabella of Mar. Isabella died soon after Marjorie was born and before Robert the Bruce became King so she never had the title of Queen. Marjorie married Walter Stewart, the 6th High Steward of Scotland, which gave rise to the House of Stewart. Her son was the first Stewart monarch, King Robert II of Scotland.

Marjorie was taken captive when 12 by England and kept in a nunnery until 18 and when Scotland won the war she was released in a prisoner exchange. She was given by her father, King Robert I (Robert the Bruce), to Walter Stewart as

The Royal Lineage

his bride in reward for his service during the war. Marjorie was a headstrong young lady and went riding while heavily pregnant. She was thrown from the horse and died. Her baby, **Robert**, was saved to become the future king.

PART II The House of Stewart

The House of Stewart is a family dynasty that ruled Scotland and England from 1371 to 1714. But their story starts much earlier than that, during the era of the first Crusade in 1020. The documented story begins in the town of Dol, in Brittany, in the Northwest of France.

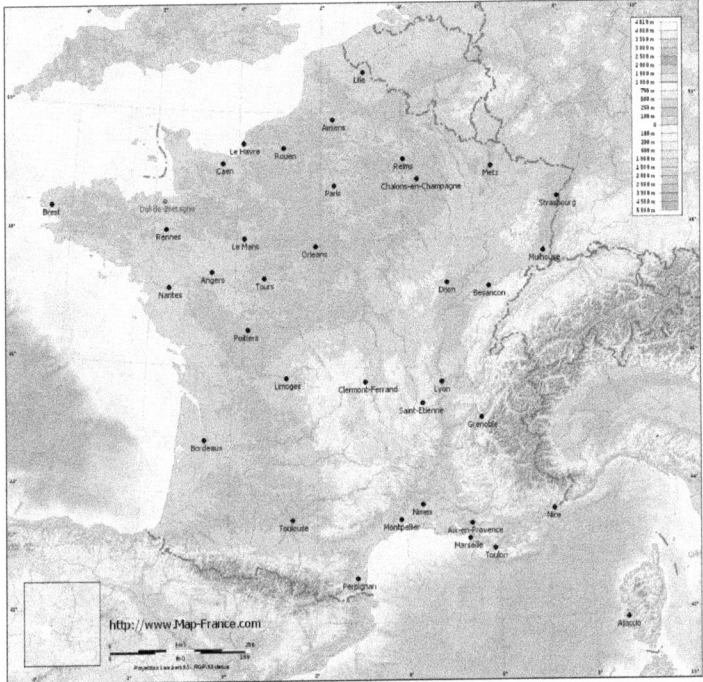

Figure 9 Map showing location of Dol

The Stewart's (also spelled Stuart) are descended from the Count of Dol, an administrator in the French aristocracy of the region, and his son, Flaad Fitzalan, who served in the first Crusade with William the Conqueror. We will trace the descendants of this family to Robert Stewart of Connecticut and from there, in Part III, to Adele Stone. It is sometimes hard to follow the line because of the titles and name changes along the way, but this is the story, as documented in the encyclopedias and history books.

Alan Dapifor of Dol 1024 to 1080

Alan, also known as the Count of Dol, was born about 1024 in Dol-et-Bretagne, Isle De Vilaine, France. He was an officer of justice (dapifor) in the region (Dapifor to the Archbishop of Dol) and a man of means in the community. He had three children: Alan Fitzalan born 1056, died 1097. **Flathald (Flaald) Fitzalan of Dol,** born in St. Floren in 1046, and Rhiwallon Fitzalan, who became an abbot in St. Floren. His eldest son Alan (also spelled Alain) was a crusader and in 1097 died in Jerusalem without leaving any children. His lands and office reverted to his brother, Flaald. All this is found in the book <u>Studies of Peerage and Family History</u> authored by J Horace Round, London 1901. The First Crusade started in 1095 when Pope Urban II called for Christian princes across Europe to launch a war against Muslims in order to reclaim the Holy Land. He promised forgiveness of sins to all who went and immediate entry into heaven for any who died for the cause. Between 60,000 and 100,000 people answered the call and joined the march on Jerusalem. In July of 1099 they were victorious in defeating the Muslims and gaining control of the Holy City. After the victory they set up several Latin Christian states but less than 50 years later the Muslim's once again conquered Jerusalem.

Figure 10 Plaque in Dol De Bretagne

Figure 11 Conquering of Jerusalem 1099

Flathald (Flaald)Fitzalan of Dol 1046 to ?

Flaald was born in 1046 in Dol-et-Bretagne, Isle De Vilaine, France. He married Domina Norton. They had at least one child, **Alan Fitzflaald**. Flaald was a knight and like his father before him he went into battle. The conflict of those times involved William, the Duke of Normandy and the son of Viking raiders. In 1060 William's cousin King Edward of England died, leaving no children, and William had to battle the English Earl Harold Godwinson for the throne. To win the throne, William built a large fleet, invaded England and defeated Harold at the Battle of Hastings. Flaad rode with William, now known as "William the Conqueror" and came to Briton as a result of this. After William became King he rewarded Flaad the barony and castle of Oswaldestre, Salop and Meleham, in Norfolk. This is how Flaad became a baron and a landowner.

Alan Fitzflaald 1085 to 1114

Alan was born about 1085 in, Shropshire, England. He followed in his father's footsteps and became a knight. He rode with William, son of William the Conqueror and King of England after his father's death. Alan, along with his father, Flaald, fought with William and Henry.. King William and his younger brother, Henry, ganged up against their brother Robert, then King of Normandy, and together they fought against him. King William died in a hunting accident in 1100 and Henry seized the throne. Alan and his father became friends with King Henry I of England who also bestowed lands and titles upon them. Alan married Aveline,(born in 1080) daughter of Ernoulf de Hesdin (who was killed on crusade at Antioch). They were married in 1098 and they had four children, Jordan, born 1101, William born 1105 died 1160, **Walter, born 1108** and Sybil, born 1115. . Alan died in 1114, at the age of 29.

As the eldest son, Jordan inherited the family estates, titles and offices. William became the Lord of Oswestrie in Shropshire. He took on younger brother **Walter** as a vassel, giving him land in return for allegiance and service.

Figure 12 King Henry defeats Robert 1106

Walter FitzAlan 1108 to 1177

Walter was born in 1108, the third son of Alan and Aveline fitzFlaald. He was described as Norman by culture and Breton by blood. He lived on the lands of brother William as a vassal, owning "two knights fees" worth of land. In a charter in 1185 he and brother William were listed as benefactors of the order of the Knights of Templars. When King Henry I died, he named his daughter Matilda as queen to succeed him (his only son had drowned in the sinking of a ship.). Her cousin, Stephen, however, wanted the throne and a state of civil war broke out. William and Walter FitzAlan sided with Empress Matilda. When it became obvious Matilda would not win, Walter befriended her uncle, King David I of Scotland. Walter went to Scotland in 1136 and fought in the civil war for Scotland in 1138 under Prince Henry, son of King David I. King David rewarded him by appointing him Steward of Scotland in 1157 and it was made a hereditary office. He was judge of the kings household and the whole family of the royal palace was under his care. Along with this appointment, he received great estates in the lowlands of Scotland. In 1164 he repelled an invasion of Renfrewshire. Walter married Eschyna de Molle, daughter of Thomas de London in 1131 in Paisley, Renfrewshire, Scotland. They had five children: Margery, born 1132, **Alan**, born 1135, Simon born 1138, Walter born ? and Christine born 1148. Walter died in 1177, at the age of 77.

Walter was given many properties by the King and at one, in Paisley, he founded Paisley Abbey for the monks in 1163. The original building was burned down, but the replacement still stands today. This was the burial place for the family for generations to come and Walter was buried here.

Figure 13 Paisley Abbey

Alan FitzWalter 1135 to 1204

Alan was born in 1135 to Walter and Eschyna FitzAlan. He was a knight and a crusader that accompanied Richard the Lionheart on the 3rd Crusade (1189-1192) and returned to Scotland in 1191. He was also the hereditary 2nd High Steward of Scotland. He was a patron of the Knights Templar and expanded the Templar influence in Scotland. He acquired the Isle of Bute and erected Rothsay Castle on the island. Alan married twice. He married Eva in 1162. They had no children. Then he married Alesta, daughter of Morggan, Earl of Mar. They had four children, David, born 1163, **Walter,** born 1165, Leonard, born 1168 and Avelina, born 1175. All were born in Paisley, Renfreshire, Scotland. Alan died in 1204 at the age of 69.

Figure 14 King Richard on the 3rd Crusade

Figure 15 Rothsay Castle

Walter Steward of DunDonald 1165 to 1246

Walter was born 1165, eldest son of Alan and Alesta FitzWalter. Instead of taking the name of his father, as was tradition, he took the name of his office. He was the first to use Stewart as a surname and was known as Steward of DunDonald. All future Stewards are descended from him. He was the 3rd hereditary High Steward of Scotland. He had the first arms of Stewart: The spelling of the name is different in different references.

In 1203 he married Bethoc Crist, daughter of Gille Crist, Earl of Angus. They had ten children, **Alexander,born 1214**, Robert,born 1218, John,born 1210, Walter, born 1212, William, Beatrix, born 1215, Christian, Eupheme, Margaret, born 1221,and Sybella.

Walter died in 1246 in DunDonald, Ayrshire, Scotland, at the age of 80.

Alexander Stewart 1214 to 1283

Alexander was born in 1214. He lived and died in DunDonald Castle, Irvine, Ayrshire, Scotland. Alexander accompanied Louis IX of France on the 7th Crusade in 1248-1254.

Figure 16 King Louis of France on the 7th Crusade

He was a commander under King Alexander III of Scotland at the Battle of Largs in 1263 when the Scots defeated the Norwegians. They had the Norwegians outnumbered and trapped by a storm so they could not get reinforcements. As soon as possible the Norwegians gave up the fight. For his service he received from the King the land and barony of Garlies.

In 1248 Alexander married Jean Macrory, daughter of James Macrory, Lord of Bute. They had at least five children: Elizabeth born 1249, **James** born 1252, John born 1256, Hawise, born 1262, and Andrew born 1266 . His son John died in the Battle of Falkirk on July 22, 1298, fighting for Sir William Wallace. Alexander died in 1283, at the age of 77.

James Stewart 1252 to 1309

James was born in 1252. He was a Scottish noble and in 1286 was appointed one of the six Regents of Scotland who had the right to appoint a king. In 1297 he submitted to King Edward I of England (known as Edward Longshanks). Yet he was one of the auditors for Robert the Bruce. During the wars of Scottish Independence he joined Sir William Wallace. After defeat at the Battle of Falkirk in 1298 he gave his support to Robert the Bruce. It is said that William Wallace's lands were in his territory and the family were his vassals. He held the hereditary post of 5th High Steward of Scotland. In 1306 he was forced to swear allegiance to King Edward I but in spite of the threat of excommunication, he joined forces again with Robert the Bruce and died in his service July 15, 1309 at age 57.

Figure 17 Battle of Falkirk

He married Cecilia daughter of Patrick of Dunbar. Later he married Gilles, daughter of Walter de Burgh in 1289. He had five children. The children were:

Andrew born 1290, **Walter**, born 1292, John born 1294, Gille born 1296, and James born 1298.

Walter Stewart 1292 to 1327

Walter was born in 1292 in DunDonald, Ayrshire, Scotland. and was the 6th High Steward of Scotland. He commanded the left wing of the Scottish army at the battle at Bannockburn in 1314. This was a defining battle in the Scottish fight for independence because they soundly routed the English, now under command of Edward II, a much weaker leader than his father. This gave the Scottish the momentum and encouragement to take back their country.

Figure 18 The Battle at Bannockburn

In 1315 he married Marjorie Bruce, (born in 1297) daughter of Robert the Bruce, who became King of Scotland in 1306, following the defeat and death of William Wallace. Marjorie herself had a very strange childhood, having been taken prisoner by King Edward I, along with her step mother and two aunts, when she was only 11. She was released in 1314 in a prisoner exchange. Walter was rewarded for his bravery in battle with the hand of Marjorie. Her dowry included the barony of Bathgate. It is said that Marjory was very headstrong and, in 1316, insisted on going riding while heavily pregnant. She was thrown from her horse on the Renfrew Road and fatally wounded. She was rushed to the Monastery where a crude caesarean was performed to save the baby. The baby, **Robert**, was born March 2, 1316. Robert survived but Marjory died and was buried in the grounds of the Paisley Monastery.

Walter remarried, to Isabelle Graham and with her had three more children, John, Andrew and Gille. As High Steward he spent much of his time defending the borders of Scotland. He was a part of many skirmishes with the English. Walter died in April 9 1327 at age 35.

Robert Stewart 1316-1390

King Robert II of Scotland

Figure 19 King Robert II

Known as King Robert II, he was born in 1316 in Paisley, Renfrewshire, Scotland, after an emergency caesarean when his mother fell from a horse. He was the son of Marjorie and Walter and grandson of Robert the Bruce. Two years after his birth the parliament of Scotland decreed that if the King

Robert I (Robert the Bruce) died without sons, Marjorie's son Robert would become King. However in 1324 King Robert I did sire a son, David, who became the next King.

Robert took part in many battles as a young man and was chosen as one of three regents of the kingdom when things became unsettled and King David had to flee to safety. Robert was able to restore order and the king was able to return in 1341. Then King David and Robert had a falling out over allowing the Scottish throne to pass to English King Edward III and Robert with four of his sons were imprisoned in 1363. When King David died childless in 1371, Robert took the throne.

Robert had at least 21 children. He married Elizabeth Mure (1320-1355) in 1336. They had eight children. With his second wife, Euphemis, he had five more children. He also had at least eight illegitimate children. His first child **John**, born 1337, was the heir to the throne.

Robert became King of Scots in 1371, at age 55, following the death of his uncle Edward, who died without children. He was the first monarch of the House of Stewart. He died in 1390 at age 74.

John Stewart 1337 to 1406

King Robert III

John was born in 1337. He was the eldest son of Robert and Elizabeth. In 1368 King David II made him Earl of Carrick. In order to solidify the Stewarts as a power in Scotland, John was made Lieutenant of the Kingdom in the north. His younger brother Alexander was Lieutenant in the south. There were many problems with this arrangement.

6 *Robert III Stewart*

Figure 20 King Robert III

He married Anabella Drommond (1350-1401), daughter of Sir John Drummond of Stobhall who was the queens's deceased brother. Robert and Annabella had seven children. David, born 1378, Robert, died in infancy, **James**, born 1394,

Margaret, Mary, Elizabeth, and Egidia who also died in infancy. He also had two illegitimate children.

John did not ascend the throne until age 53. When his grand uncle, King David II died childless Robert's father Robert II became king. There was much intrigue and maneuvering in ruling the kingdom, but then Robert II died in 1390 and John became King. He changed his name in 1390 to Robert to maintain the line. He was described as feeble, timid and unfit to rule. He had been crippled as a result of a riding accident two years before he came to the throne. He had a reputation for kindliness and justice. His personal qualities and failing health undermined his authority and power and his brother, Robert Stewart known as the Duke of Albany, and his eldest son, David, the Duke of Rothesay were given the power. Albany imprisoned Rothesay in Falkland Palace where he starved to death in 1402. Robert III then sent his younger son, James to France for safety, but he was captured and became a prisoner of King Henry IV. King Robert III died April 4, 1406 at age 69 and described himself as the worst of kings and most miserable of men. He is buried in Paisley Abbey.

James Stewart 1394 to 1437

King James I of Scotland

James was born Dec 10, 1394 in Edinburgh Castle. His father, Robert III, feared for his safety due to plots by his uncle, Robert Stuart, 1st Duke of Albany, who may have already killed James' older brother. James was sent to France for safety but was captured enroute by the English and held prisoner until 1424. This allowed the Duke of Albany to rule when Robert III died in 1406 and his son after his death. A number of nobles, including Archibald Douglas finally arranged his ransom in 1424. During his captivity he had been well educated and treated as a royal guest. He is said to have a love of literature.

Figure 21 King James I

He married Joan Beaufort (1398-1445), daughter of the Earl of Somerset before leaving England. They had eight children, 6 daughters and a son, **James** (who was a twin but his brother died in infancy). Upon taking control in May 1424, he asserted his authority and ruthlessly exterminated members of the Albany family and other barons and brought order to the clans. He achieved financial and judicial reforms and remodeled the Scottish Parliament along English lines. Some of his policies were unpopular and he was assassinated by a group of nobles. He died Feb 21,1437 at the age of 43.

James Stewart 1430 to 1460

King James II

James was born in October 16, 1430 at Holyrood Palace in Edinburgh. He was a twin but his brother, Alexander, died in infancy. He became king in 1437 (at age 7) on the death of his father and was crowned a month later on 25 March. As usual, the time of the regency was one of civil discord; the Douglas' were then very powerful, one of them being regent.

After the death of the regent in 1439, Sir Alexander Livingston of Callendar imprisoned James' mother Queen Joan and her new husband in Stirling Castle and only released them when he was given custody of the king until he became of age. James was known as "fiery face" due to a vermillion birthmark on his face.

Figure 22 James became King at age 7

James became King at age 7

The power of the Douglas' was further reduced in 1440 when they were invited to what became known as the "Black Dinner" in Edinburgh Castle attended by the ten-year-old King James. His cousins, the young Earl of Douglas and his brother were murdered on the orders of the governor of the castle, Sir William Crichton, a member of another powerful family. Sir Alexander Livingston was also implicated in the crime.

James married Mary, daughter of the duke of Gueldres, in 1449 when he was 19 and she was 15.. She was French and Included in her dowry were cannons which were superior to anything known in Scotland at that time. The marriage improved relations between Scotland and France. They had seven children. Of his four sons, the eldest, **James** became the next king.

Figure 23 King James II

In 1449. At age 19, James assumed power and realized he had to fight the acting rulers, Livingston, Douglas and Ross to get control of the country. One of his first acts was to imprison Sir Alexander Livingston and forfeit his lands. James then invited the 8th Earl of Douglas to Stirling Castle and requested him to break his liaison with the Earl of Ross and the Lord of the Isles. When Douglas refused, James stabbed him and his bodyguard killed him.

Although the murder resulted in a civil war, James was successful in quelling the conflict - those cannons gifted as part of the dowry came in useful. In 1455 Parliament forfeited the Douglas estates and a number of the Douglas castles became crown property.

James became involved in a war with England and it was while he was participating in a siege of Roxburgh Castle in 1460 that he was killed, at the young age of 30. He is buried in Holyrood Abbey.

Figure 24 Holyrood Abbey

James Stewart, 1451 to 1488

King James III

James was born in 1451 and crowned king in 1460 at 9 years of age when his father, James II, was killed in an accident involving an exploding cannon. The queen mother, Mary of Gueldres, was appointed Regent and was aided in government by Bishop Kennedy. When Bishop Kennedy died the powerful magnates led by Sir Alexander Boyd, kidnapped the child king and forced him to appoint them as guardian.

Figure 25 James Stewart crowned King at age 9

King James himself was arranged to be married to Princess Margaret of Denmark. They were married at Holyrood Abbey in July 1469, when he was 18. For a dowry the King of Denmark pledged the lands of Orkney and Shetland. James and Margaret had three sons. After his marriage he began to assert himself in government but was easily influenced by others. He was artistic and sensitive and not a strong ruler.

Figure 26 King James III

The people of Scotland blamed him for poor harvests, famine, plague and inflation. He survived imprisonment by his brother and an uprising as his brother Alexander, the Duke of Albany attempted to sieze the crown, with the help of King Edward IV of England. Having regained control he returned to music, riding and hunting instead of governing the country. He became estranged from his wife and also his eldest son, **James**, due to his preference for his younger son. There was another rebellion at Sauchieburn and the King and his army rode out to meet the rebels bearing the sword of his ancestor Robert the Bruce. Unfortunately he was defeated and killed either in the battle or shortly afterwards in 1488 at age 37.

James Stewart 1473 to 1513

King James IV

James was born in 1473 and took the throne in June 11, 1488, when his father was killed in the Battle of Sauchieburn. He was 15. James learned that the rebels used him indirectly in the death of his father and from them on wore a heavy chain around his waist next to the skin each Lent as penance.

Figure 27 King James IV crowned at age 15

He was known as a successful monarch who did much to advance learning and culture. He spoke at least six languages, including Gaelic. He was a true Renaissance prince with an interest in practical and scientific matters. He granted the Edinburgh College of Surgeons a royal charter in 1506, turned Edinburgh Castle into one of Britian's formost gun foundries and welcomed the establishment of Scotland's first printing press in 1505. .He believed Scotland needed a strong maritime presence and had built a fleet of ships.

He married Margaret Tudor in 1503 and they had six children. **James** was the only one to survive past one year of age. He also had eight illegitimate children with four different mistresses. He died at the Battle of Flodden Field in Sept 9, 1513 at the age of 40.

James Stewart 1512 to 1542

King James V

James Stewart, King James V was born in 1512. James became King at the age of 17 months. After his father's was killed at the battle of Flodden against the English, His mother, Margaret Tudor, was to be crowned so long as she remained unwed. She remarried in 1514 to Archbald Douglas, the 6th Earl of Angus, who took control of the boy king and the realm until James became old enough to run him out of Scotland. James hated his step-father. There was much bickering in the realm for control to the point that the Scottish called in John Stuart the Duke of Albany from France to take temporary control and restore order. This was vehemently opposed by his mother but to his credit Stuart made no effort to overthrow the young king and merely tried to stabilize the regime.

The Royal Lineage

John Stuart expelled Margaret Tudor, his mother, who could no longer be considered Regent since she had remarried. When he returned to France in 1522, Henry VIII sent troops to burn and plunder the Borders. Albany returned with French troops and drove the English out but returned again to France and then fighting broke out among the Scottish nobles. In 1524 after Albany had left, Henry VIII arranged it that 12 year old James be found fit to govern, on the condition he be advised by his mother and council. His step-father effectively kept him confined from 1526 to 1528, when he managed to escape and put out an order to execute the earl. He continued to war against the English until finally signing a peace treaty in 1534. He married Madeline, daughter of the King of France, in 1537, when he was 25. She was in poor health and she died shortly after arriving in Scotland.

Figure 28 King James V crowned at age 17 months

He then married another French noblewoman, Mary of Guise in 1538. Mary had two sons by a previous marriage and this union produced two sons, but both died young. Their only surviving child was Mary, born in 1542. He took a mistress, Elizabeth Carmicheal, daughter of Sir John Carmicheal. With her he had a son, **John Stewart**. James had at least nine illegitimate children, at least three of which he fathered before he was 20.

James was called "King of the Commons" because he traveled around the country at times posing as a commoner. He is said to have a wonderful singing voice but his speaking voice was harsh.

He aligned himself with the enemies of England and again England invaded. After suffering a serious defeat to the English he collapsed and was on his deathbed when his daughter was born. His daughter Mary was born December 8 and he died December 15, 1542. His infant daughter acceded to the throne and when she came of age was known as Mary, Queen of Scots.

John Stewart 1531 to 1563

Our family tree diverges from the kings and queens in this generation. John was born in 1531 and was the illegitimate son of King James V of Scotland by his mistress Elizabeth Carmichael. John Stewart was made Commendator of the Priory of Coldingham in 1541, when he seems to have been in his eighth or ninth year. This title is the head of the Benedictine monastic community. He renounced the Catholic old faith and joined the Protestant Reformers in 1560. He married Lady Jean Hepburn, daughter of the 3rd Earl of Bothwell on January 1561-2. Lady Jean's brother James was third husband to Mary, Queen of Scots. This marriage gave John title to the forfeited domains of the Earl of Lennox and the title 1st Lord Darnley. They had a son, **Francis** in 1562. John died at Inverness, probably in October or November 1563,at the age of 32.

Figure 29 Inverness Castle

Francis Stewart 1562 to 1613

Francis was born in 1562 in his mother's tower house at Morham. Francis' father died when he was an infant.. He was given Crichton Castle by King James VI, when he was 18, on June 16, 1581, and he was also awarded the title of 1st Earl of Bothwell.

Figure 30 Crichton Castle

The new Earl of Bothwell was described as wild and dangerous. He made frequent trips abroad and was impressed with the European Renaissance style. In 1585 he renovated Crichton with new kitchens, living quarters, colonades, dining room and drawing rooms. He had installed a very modern straight stairway with landings. This castle still stands today and is open for touring. Francis' flamboyant decorative additions make it one of the most interesting Scottish castles. He was a big spender, which caused his heirs to inherit his debt and eventually lose his properties. He held the office of Governor of the Realm in 1589.

When he was 15, he married Lady Margaret Douglas on Dec 1 1577 at Crichton Castle in Midlothian, Scotland. Initially, after a brief honeymoon, the new earl was not permitted to come within twenty miles of his new wife because he was too young. They later had, at least, four sons and four daughters. **Francis**, born in 1584, was his eldest. He engaged in witchcraft and was known by the nickname of "Wizard Earl". At first he was a favorite of the King. But then he was accused of conspiracy and on June 2, 1591 he was imprisoned for witchcraft. He escaped June 22 and on June 25 was stripped of his title and lands. On Dec 27 he tried to kidnap the King at Holyrood to negotiate his reinstatement, but failed. A year and a half later, on July 17 1593, he again tried to kidnap the king at Falkland. Four days later Parliament removed his rights and he fled. The following April 3 he appeared with 500 horsemen but achieved nothing, and then fled to England and on to France, Spain and Italy. He died in exile on Nov 4, 1613.

Francis Stewart, 2nd Earl of Bothwell 1584 to 1640

Francis was born into royalty in 1584 and although his father was stripped of his title before his death, Francis still called himself Earl Bothwell or Lord Stewart. He was the 2nd Earl of Bothwell, since his father was known as the 1st Earl of Bothwell and the title passed down through the generations . His father's title was reinstated for him, but he laboured under his father's debts, and sold Crichton Castle to the Hepburns of Humbie. He obtained the Priory of Coldingham from his brother John, but it was in debt. He married Lady Isobel Seton (1593-1638), daughter of Sir Robert Seton, 1st Earl of Winton. He was able to regain some of his rights through this connection by 1633. He then sold part of the family estates to the Winston family. He basically lost his fortune and was barely scraping by and had to petition King Charles I to be made Printer to the King of Ireland. When he died in 1640 his son Robert inherited his debts

Figure 31 Priory of Coldingham

Robert Stewart 1636 to 1688

Robert was born in Scotland in 1636, the son of royalty but the family fortune had been squandered. Robert inherited a barony title but also huge family debts. After a long struggle he lost the Barony of Coldingham to the Renton family. He supported his homeland, Scotland by fighting in the Battle of Worcester against the English. The English won that battle and Robert became a prisoner of war. The English decided a good use of prisoners was as slave labor in the lumber mills and mines of the colonies. Robert appears on the list of prisoners sent to the colonies in 1652, on the *John and Sarah* of London.

Part III American Ancestry

1652 to Present

Robert Stewart 1636 to 1688

In 1652 Captain John Greene anchored his ship, the John and Sara in Boston Harbor after a long winter crossing of the North Atlantic. As told in the book by Diane Rapaport, The Fate of the Scottish Prisoners in 17th Century Massachusettes, 2002, the ship was carrying 300 Scottish prisoners from the English Civil War. A list of these prisoners was recorded as they unloaded the ship and filed in Boston with the Suffolk Recorder of Deeds. Robert Stewart is on this list.

The good puritans of Massachusetts were apparently more than happy to have slave labor. According to various town records, "Scotchmen" occupied an inferior social status along with "Negroes" and "Indians".

Once in America he was first documented in Milford, Connecticut. Many of the prisoners settled in Kittery and Lynn (now Berwick) Maine. After working off his indenture, which typically lasted seven years, Robert settled in Norwalk, CT and married Bethia Rumble on June 12, 1661, when he was 25 and she was 20. They had 10 children, **James** being the oldest. The location of their home in Norwalk is shown on this old map of Norwalk:

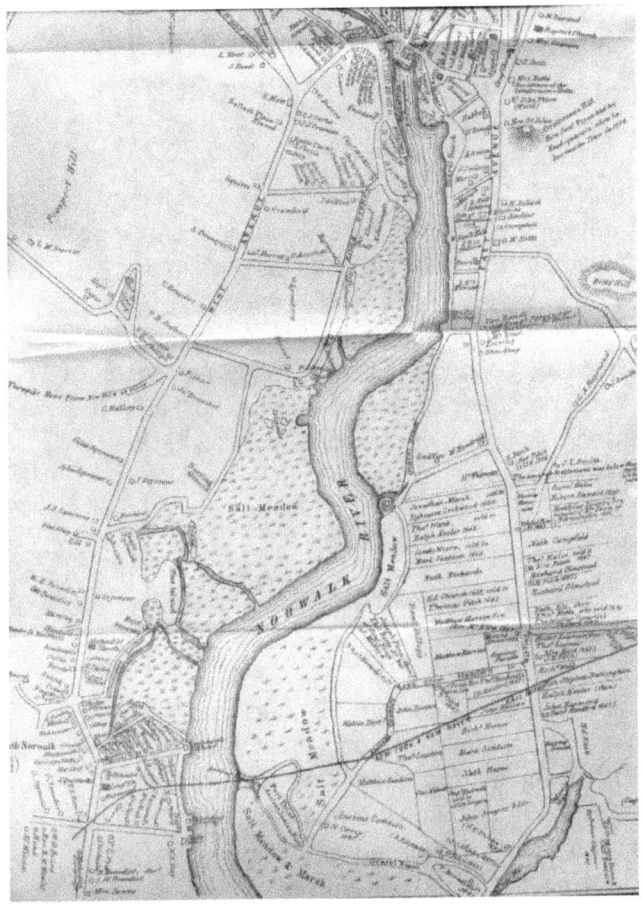

Figure 32 Robert Stewart home on map of Norwalk

Robert died Dec 5, 1688, at the age of 52.

James Stewart 1663 to 1751

James was born March 19, 1663 in Norwalk, CT. His father was a Scottish immigrant brought over as a prisoner of war by the British, as noted above. He was the oldest child in a family of 3 boys and 7 girls. He married Experience in 1694. They had six children, four girls and two boys. They must have lived in Westport, Connecticut before 1699 since second child, Hannah was born there. **Deborah** was the next to youngest child and was born in Stratford, Connecticut. James died June 12, 1751 in Norwalk, at age 88.

Deborah Stewart 1706 to 1756

Deborah was born in 1706 in Stratford, Connecticut. She was married April 14, 1726 to James Pickett, son of John Pickett of Norwalk, CT. They had six children, 3 boys and 3 girls. The youngest was **Ezra**. Deborah was the daughter of James Stewart (1663-1751) and Experience (1666-1765) of Norwalk, Connecticut. Deborah died in 1756 in Norwalk at age 50.

Ezra Picket 1740 to 1799

Ezra was born July 12, 1740 in Norwalk, CT. He married Elizabeth Benedict March 30, 1761. He was the son of James Pickett (1703-1799) of Norwalk, Connecticut and

Deborah Stewart (1706-1756) of Stratford, Connecticut. Ezra and Elizabeth had a daughter, **Elizabeth** on Jan 14, 1769 in Norwalk, CT. Ezra died in Nov, 1799 in Norwalk, CT at age 59.

Elizabeth Picket Quintard 1769 to 1818

Elizabeth, the only known child of Ezra and Elizabeth Picket of Norwalk, CT married Isaac Quintard of Stamford, CT on Nov 13, 1793 when she was 24. Isaac Quintard was born April 28, 1764 in Stamford, CT. Isaac was the son of Peter Quintard, a sergeant the Connecticut troops in the Revolutionary War. Isaac was a land owner in the time that the colonies were controlled by the crown: He was a pottery maker and also ran a market sloop to New York. They had seven children, five boys and two girls. **Charles** was number four. Elizabeth died in 1818 at age 49 and Isaac later remarried. Isaac died Nov 4, 1855 at age 91.

Charles Quintard 1800 to 1850

Charles was born April 19, 1800 in Norwalk, Connecticut, the fourth of seven children. Through his father Isaac and grandfather Peter he can trace his lineage back to Isaac Quintard of Lusignan, France and to silversmith Peter Quintard of New York

Figure 33 Peter Quintard made this tankard

In 1822, Charles married Maria Jelliffe, also of Norwalk. By 1850 they had moved with their six children to Miller, Ohio. **Emeline Maria** was the oldest, born June 3, 1823 in Norwalk, CT. Charles died in 1850 at age 50.

After the death of her husband, Maria lived with her youngest daughter, Martha. Even after Martha married to Charles Cooper, she lived with them in Buckingham, Iowa. Later she moved in with daughter Sarah Hall in Iowa. Maria died in 1891 at age 87.

Figure 34 Maria Quintard grave in Woodlawn Cemetary Toledo OH

Emeline Maria Quintard Tuttle 1823 to 1893

Emiline was born June 3, 1823 in Norwalk, Connecticut, the oldest of seven children of Charles and Maria Quintard. Her parents moved to Ohio after 1845 where she met Isaac Tuttle and married him in 1851. Emilene and Isaac had three children, **Rose** being the middle child. They later moved to Bethlehem, Indiana. Both Isaac and Emeline died in Hebron, Indiana, she at the age of 70 and he at 77.

Side note: Maria was the daughter of James Jelliffe, who Served as private, in 1780 in Capt. Eliphalet Lockwood's company of Connecticut coast guards. Another revolutionary war veteran in the family tree. But I digress.

Rose Emilene DeTuttle Shively Lewis 1865 to 1947

Born June 29, 1865 in Ohio, Emiline was the daughter of Isaac DeTuttle of Greene Pennsylvania (1812-1890) and Emeline Maria Quintard of Norwalk, Connecticut (1823-1894). Census reports show her name as Francis Rose Tuttle but later she is called Rose Emeline DeTuttle. She must have changed her name along the way. She married Leander Shivley when she was 17 in Rochester, Indiana. They had 12 children and came to Spokane in 1907.

Figure 35 Shively family at restaurant

Leander and Emma Shively had a restaurant/bakery on the corner of Madelia and Sprague in Spokane in the early 1900's.

Figure 36 Shively famly 1907. Emma and Leander are seated in front. Nellie is front and center

Family Photo of the Shivelys: 1907 Emma and Leander are seated in front. Nellie is front and center.

They led an interesting life which is detailed at the end of this story by her granddaughter, Lolabelle. When Leander died in 1935, she married John Lewis. She was run over and killed on the streets of Spokane Dec 30, 1947 at the age of 82.

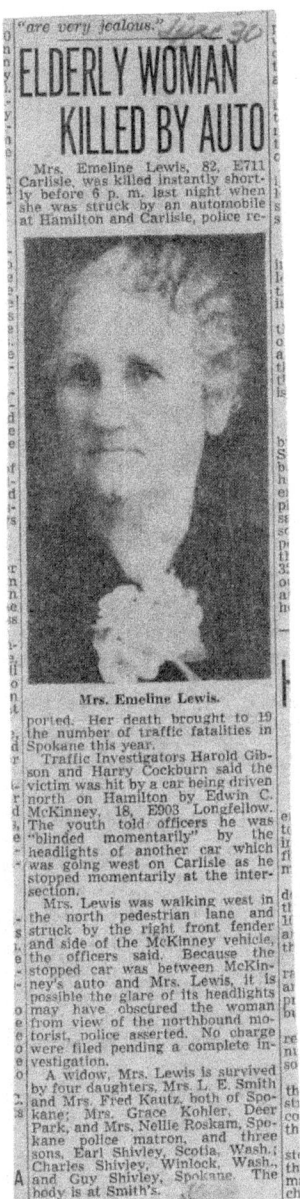

"are very jealous." June 36

ELDERLY WOMAN KILLED BY AUTO

Mrs. Emeline Lewis, 82, E711 Carlisle, was killed instantly shortly before 6 p. m. last night when she was struck by an automobile at Hamilton and Carlisle, police re-

Mrs. Emeline Lewis.

ported. Her death brought to 19 the number of traffic fatalities in Spokane this year.

Traffic Investigators Harold Gibson and Harry Cockburn said the victim was hit by a car being driven north on Hamilton by Edwin C. McKinney, 18, E903 Longfellow. The youth told officers he was "blinded momentarily" by the headlights of another car which was going west on Carlisle as he stopped momentarily at the intersection.

Mrs. Lewis was walking west in the north pedestrian lane and struck by the right front fender and side of the McKinney vehicle, the officers said. Because the stopped car was between McKinney's auto and Mrs. Lewis, it is possible the glare of its headlights may have obscured the woman from view of the northbound motorist, police asserted. No charge were filed pending a complete investigation.

A widow, Mrs. Lewis is survived by four daughters, Mrs. L. E. Smith and Mrs. Fred Kautz, both of Spokane; Mrs. Grace Kohler, Deer Park, and Mrs. Nellie Roskam, Spokane police matron, and three sons, Earl Shivley, Scotia, Wash.; Charles Shivley, Winlock, Wash., and Guy Shivley, Spokane. The body is at Smith's.

Nellie Shively Palmer Roskam 1900to 1997

Nellie was born Aug 25, 1900 to Leander Shively and Rose Emaline DeTuttle Shively, in New Auburn, Wisconsin, the ninth of 12 children. When she was 7, her family moved to Spokane, and within a few years were running a restaurant and bakery near Madelia and Sprague. Stories of the early years in the Leander Shively family were written down by granddaughter Lolabelle, Erl's daughter. It is included at the end of this document.

Nellie married Fred Ival Palmer In January 1917 in Coeur D'Alene, Idaho just across the state line from Spokane. They had two children, Adele Elizabeth, born Feb 4, 1918 and Alfred Eugene born April 18, 1919 both in Spokane.

Figure 37 Nellie and Fred Palmer with Al and Adele 1920

Nellie and Fred divorced and Fred remarried in 1926 and moved first to Livingston, Montana and then to Denver Colorado. He had 6 children by his second wife, while living in the Denver area.

Nellie also remarried, in 1930, to Arie Roskam, from the Netherlands. More information about Nellie's life as a young single parent is found in Adele's Story.

Figure 38 Arie and Nellie Roskam

Arie and Nellie

Nellie and Harry continued living in Spokane. Nellie lived to be 96 years old.

Adele Elizabeth Palmer Stone 1918 to 2003

Adele was born Feb 4, 1918 in Spokane. She was the daughter of Fred Ival Palmer (1894-1981) and Nellie Shively (1900-1997).

Figure 39 Al and Adele Palmer

Adele had a younger brother, Alfred (later changed to Al), who later moved to the Sea Tac area to raise his family. It is unusual to get a detailed account of a relative's life. We were fortunate that Adele wrote the story of her life as a girl and young wife and it is included at the end of this document.

Figure 40 Adele Palmer

Adele and her husband Gene raised six children and kept the family together through holiday gatherings that almost everyone attended.

Figure 41 Gene and Adele with children Gene, Joan, Judy, Butch, Linda and John

Sadly the tradition has not continued after her death in 2003, at the age of 85.

The Shively Story

The first we know of the Shivley family we find them in the Indiana census of 1860. John Shivley is married to Margaret____. We see by the census that they were both born in Pennsylvania, we don't know where. Their son James lives close by. He is married to Catharine Glaze and Leander is seven at this time, having been born in Indiana.

In 1882 Leander married Rose Emeline Tuttle we think in Rochester, Indiana because their first son Erl was born there in 1885. When he was a baby they moved to a farm in the Bass Lake district in Wisconsin about five miles from Chetek, near Prairie Lake.

They homesteaded forty acres of good farm land and bought eighty acres more later. Crops were good and the corn grew night and day because it was so hot in the summer. The weather was very changeable though. They would be out cutting hay and a little cloud would come up and before they could unhitch the horses and get to the barn it would be pouring rain.

Aunt Grace told of one time her folks had gone to visit some neighbors and left the kids at home. Charlie, Clint and Grace were supposed to cultivate the garden. Clint drove the horse which was trained to walk down between the rows without walking on the plants. Grace and Charlie were supposed to pull the weeds around the plants. They hurried to get through so they could play croquet. Erl had made them a croquet set. They had just got the game set up when all at once it got real dark and it was still early afternoon. So they gathered up the croquet set and went in the house. The wind came up and they had a regular cyclone. Erl opened the door to look outside and it took all four of them to close the door again. Erl then took a piece of wood out of the wood box and nailed it across the door opening to keep the wind from breaking the latch. Their folks couldn't come until the storm was over. They had terrible storms in summer and after a storm it was just as hot as before.

In the winter it was very cold, but they never needed boots as the weather was a dry cold. Most of the time it was below zero. In January of 1904 their house burned. The kids had been playing up in the attic and they figured the kids must have got some papers or things next to the hot stove. Charlie was out doing the chores and he saw the fire coming out of the roof. Their folks weren't home and Grace, being the oldest, grabbed the quilts off the beds and carried the little ones out in the snow and wrapped the quilts around them. Their folks saw the fire from the neighbors but by the time they got there they had lost nearly everything, but no lives were lost. The neighbors helped them out every way they could, even helped them build a new house on the eighty acres near the road.

Now they had their mail delivered from New Auburn, where before they had to go to town for it. The mother made butter and sold it. Later they sold milk to a cheese factory. It was lots of work keeping the milk cans washed and delivering the milk.

There were nine children in the family that grew up. At least two children died between Erl and Clint. One little boy died ofsmall pox, and a little girl, six year old Coral, died in an accident, (she tried to put kerosene in a hot stove.)

The father, Leander, was an engineer. He fired engines for mills and worked on threshing machines during harvest. Erl being the oldest son, worked around doing odd jobs for the neighbors, cutting wood, logging and doing other things. One winter he worked unloading fish on Lake Superior.

One winter he came home and his Dad had written on the window in the frost,"Spokane or Bust". Everyone was sick, in fact that was one of the reasons they decided to sell. The other reason being the terrible storms and they heard the weather was much better in Spokane.

The Royal Lineage

On June 6, 1907, their Dad having sold their farm, they went first to New Auburn, then Chetekrand, from there to St. Paul, where they boarded the train for Spokane. When they got on the train, Clint took a seat with Ida, Charlie sat with Fay, and Grace took care of Nellie. Their folks had two facing seats and they took the two little ones, Guy and Hugh with them. They were on the train three and a half days and three and a half nights. Erl came on a rented train box car with the furniture and stock. They had two cows and two horses and a colt. They had a wagon, an organ and some beds and not much more.

They got to Spokane at twelve o'clock at night. The man at the depot took them to a hotel on Monroe and Main, where they all shared the same room, the parents sleeping in the bed and the kids slept on the floor.

They soon found a place to rent about where Krause Nursery is today. It was all farms then. The neighbors gave the folks a bed, and the kids slept on the floor, for three weeks until the train car with Erl came.

About the middle of August they bought a place in Williams Valley, near Deer Park. Ida, Fay, and Nellie went to school at Happy Homes School. Later a new school was built nearby called Boughs School. It was while they lived here that Grace became acquainted with Emil Koehler, and was married in November in 1908, at the age of seventeen. She was the first break in the family.

About this time he family moved to Wild Rose Prairie. After living there a while the folks left the kids with the older brothers and sisters and started a restaurant on Sprague, not far from Division. I guess it wasn't very successful, so they rejoined the family on the farm.

After a while the whole family moved to the corner of Madelia and Sprague, where they had a combination restaurant and bakery . Erl baked the bread and pies, and his mother with the help of the others ran the restaurant. They lived in rooms above the restaurant.

In 1912, the family moved to 4524 West Crown, just off Northwest Boulevard. Here they slept in tents and cooked in a small shed, while they started to build a house. In 1990 the house still stands.

The mother and two daughters, Fay and Ida got jobs in the Washington Laundry. It was here that they met Emma Christofferson who worked there as a starcher. On April 13, 1914, Clint Shivley and Emma Christofferson were married. They had two children, Milton born 1915, and Clayton born 1916. These boys lost both parents in the Flu Epidemic of 1919 and were raised by the Shivley Grandparents.

In 1915 Erl Shivley married Minnie Eilmes. At first they lived in a little house on Alameda Street. Then Erl's folks moved from their big house on 4524 West Crown to a

Prune Ranch south of Spokane. Erl and Minnie then moved into the folks' house and began construction on a new house of their own next door.

At this time Ida and her husband Lorne Smith were living in a small house on the west side of her parent's house on Crown.

The Prune Ranch was located toward Spangle from Spokane. It consisted of several acres of fruit trees, mostly prunes, also some farm land. When the fruit was ready, the whole family and all their children gathered to give a hand. In spite of family help the venture failed so they moved back to town.

In 1921, Erl and his parents bought adjoining land at Diamond Lake. Part of the land his folks bought was the former Beyersdorf Lumber Mill site, which consisted of several buildings near the lake front. A natural ravine on the property gave easy entrance to the lake. At one time this road was used to transport logs from across the lake to the mill. A railroad track at one time led into the lake at this point and a long suspension bridge at one time spanned the ravine. It has since become the only public access to Diamond Lake.

Erl's parents moved into a house across the road from the lake. Here they had the only phone on Diamond Lake so had to run a regular messenger service for lake residents.

They also delivered milk, eggs, stove wood and fresh vegetables to lake dwellers. At the lake they rented boats, bathing suits and the lake provided ice that was cut and put up for sale and their own use. Times were hard but they lived there until 1933, when the Lee Shivley and their two grandsons moved to Spokane.

In the Spring of 1935, Leander died of a stroke, leaving his wife Emeline to survive him until 1947, when she was killed by a car. After Leanders death she lived with her two grandsons until she met John Lewis. She met him at Senior Citizens meetings. They were married in the fall of 1937, and we all became acquainted with the Lewis's and Roloff's. The family who are left are scattered around, but they all live in Washington, or did at this writing.

This family has not been very successful about male heirs to carry on the Shivley name. Erl Shivley's son Bob had a son John Robert born 1953 and he now has two sons ; John Robert Jr. and a son Robert, also a daughter Laura. So we hope the name will go on in that line.

Adele's Story

My folks lived at my fathers parents (the Palmers) house on Euclid Ave in Spokane. This was a two story house in a residential neighborhood. My grandparents had two homes, this one in Spokane and also one in Blanchard, which was a homestead. At that time my Dad, Fred Palmer, worked in a sawmill near Post Street in Spokane. While living there, I was born on February 4, 1918. My mother told me I was born on the dining room table. In those days the doctor came to your home to deliver babies. My brother Fred was born one year and two months later at the same house. When he was just a baby we had pictures taken the front yard of this house where my brother and I were sitting in a cart that was pulled by a goat. This picture was dated 1919. We also had pictures taken in an airplane in the yard. These were done by professional photographers that went around the neighborhood taking pictures.

My Mom and Dad had eloped to Coeur D' Alene Idaho to get married. My Mom's mom, Emaline Shivley, was very upset and forbid my Grandfather, Leander, to visit us. But he would sneak over to see us anyway. One time he brought some red material for my mother to sew me a dress.

We stayed in Blanchard at times. I have a picture of my mother hanging out my diapers on the fence at this home. According to Mom, I caught typhoid fever when we were there and I was so sick I couldn't even lift up my hand to take some pennies from the Doctor. The Doctor held pennies in his hand to coax me to try to raise my arm so he would know how strong I was.

The Royal Lineage

I remember one time I was told to watch my brother while he was sitting in his high chair. The next thing I remember he was on the floor underneath the high chair. I guess I was too young to watch him very well.

We later lived in a four plex on Oak Street, a one story wooden house, off Broadway near downtown Spokane. I remember making mud pies out of rotten eggs with my brother. My mother accused us of hiding the eggs so that they spoiled. Al and I had a bed in the front room. We both had the measles at the same time. My Dad had a car that he worked on in the backyard. When I was about four, I was trying to "help" out with the car. I put my hand on the wheel and it slipped and I caught my finger in the cogs. They took me to Aunt Ida's doctor. My finger was badly injured and I still have scars from this accident.

I played with a little girl down the street. I had a little doll buggy that I loved to play with. One day I had a spool of my mother's thread in the buggy. I left the buggy out on the porch while we were gone. When I returned, the buggy was gone. We looked all over the neighborhood but could not find the buggy. I was very upset, and was more worried about the loss of the thread than my buggy.

I remember one Halloween we made Jack o Lanterns. We held up our lighted pumpkin to window of our neighbor's house. He was reading the newspaper and he looked up and saw the Jack o Lantern. He jumped up and ran into the other room. We thought we had scared him and were real pleased with ourselves. We used whatever was available for toys those days. Fred played cows and sheep with red and green shotgun shell casings. My Dad worked at the Crescent Department store, the largest department store in Spokane at that time, in the fur department with Uncle Loren. He was a furrier, making coats, hats, shawls and other items out of fur.

When I was about four or five, my Mom and Dad separated. There were mother in law problems and the two arguing sets of grandparents probably contributed to the separation. My Dad went work in Montana. He came back for visits once in a while. Once he brought me a little miniature wood cook stove, complete with an opening oven. I used to bake jelly beans in this oven when I played. I have kept this oven to this day.

We lived at Uncle Earl's house in Scotia one winter. He had a one room house on a farm. We.were taking care of his house while he lived down at the store at Diamond Lake. There was an outside pump for water, an outhouse, a wood stove for cooking and heating, and kerosene lamps. We ironed clothes with flatirons heated on top of stove. A removable handle was placed in the iron to take it off the stove and iron with it. It was a cold winter with a lot of snow.

I started school at the Finch School in Spokane, which was grades one through four. I was six years old. I walked to school. I was in the A class, the newest group of first graders, first semester. I was living at Aunt Ida's, since my mother had gone to Coeur D Alene to look for work. My brother went to live with Aunt Fay at this time. My Mom found work as a waitress in a restaurant, at the Houck's Cafe in Coeur d'Alene. My brother and I again lived with my Mom, this time in a boarding house on Officer's row at Fort Sherman in Coeur d'Alene. We shared the house with Mrs. Macahome, a grandmother, and her six grandkids. They were older than us and made us do chores while they played. We went to the first grade at Sherman School, which was right across the Street from the house. One of the girls from the boarding house

The Royal Lineage

was in my class and used to make faces at me when I was reciting in school.

Mom had to walk to work through Coeur d' Alene park. One night while mom was walking home from work through the park she saw the reflection from a cigarette in the only clump of trees in the park. This scared her and went back to town and got the police to walk her home. I was advanced to the second grade.

A woodcarver lived close by. We would take pieces of wood we saved over to him and he would carve us chains from the wood. He did that to entertain us kids. Fred fell in love with his first grade teacher, Miss Queen, who was a pretty girl with long blonde hair.

On Saturdays and Sundays, we went to the Dream Theater one day and the Liberty Theater the next day to watch silent movies. They had matinees for kids, with cartoons and cowboy shows like Tom Mix and Hoot Gibson. It was very inexpensive and sometimes they even let us in for free. The piano player helped with sound effects like when there were horses running.

Qn holidays and summer vacations we went to Spokane to visit Aunt Ida and Uncle Loren or Aunt Fay and Uncle Fred, or sometimes we went to Diamond Lake to stay with Grandma and Grandpa Shively on their farm. Christmas was alternated between Aunt Ida and Aunt Fay. The whole family would get together and have a big meal and exchange gifts. One special Chistmas gift I remember was when I received a special doll from mother with a leather body and china head and my uncle Loren made me a doll bed. Aunt Ida made a dress for the doll, and sheets for the bed and Aunt Fay made a blanket to wrap the doll in. Fred and I slept in a fold out bed in the living room, The tree

The Royal Lineage

was next to this bed. Our old long stockings would be hung on the sides of our bed on Christmas Eve. In the morning, there would be new stockings in their place. The type of stockings worn on those days came up above the knees and garter belts were used to hold them up. The big Christmas tree was decorated with popcorn and cranberries and red, white and blue strips of paper. Paper chains were also used. There were candles in little candle holders, but they didn't light the candles because they were a fire hazard. Everyone wore their nice clothes.

My uncle Loren always made venison jerky. Every year they went deer hunting on the farm at Diamond Lake. In the fall there would be strips of venison hanging on racks above the heater. Once as a joke, they gave Al a piece to eat that had a string on it that was tied to the bed so we wouldn't choke on it.

Aunt Ida's house on 2908 West Rockwell, had an outhouse. The Sears catalog was the only toilet paper. There was running water in the house. She washed clothes on a washboard. She had an icebox on the porch. An iceman would come to deliver ice. We took baths in a washtub in the kitchen. The water was heated on an old wood stove. They had electric lights. They had a big beautiful garden that everyone helped out in. They also raised chickens and ducks for meat and eggs. The mail carrier had a horse and cart. The milkman also used a team of horses to deliver milk in bottles. They went down the alley and left the milk on your back porch.

I remember one time when Fred and I were at Aunt Ida's and the phone rang. We had never talked on the phone before, so we ran across the alley to the Billavecks house to have someone come over to answer the phone.

The Royal Lineage

The Indians used to gather near my Aunt Ida's house on Longfellow Street in teepees. We could see them from my Aunt's backyard.

We boarded at another house in Coeur d'Alene also, where they fed us canned milk diluted with hot water for our cereal and to drink. We did not like this and were glad to leave this place. We attended Roosevelt School in the second grade.

Once we lived next door to the chief of police, Mike Roach, in Coeur D' Alene and attended Central School. The lady of this house, who worked with Mom and her husband, was mean. Once someone left a May basket on their porch for Al and me and she threw them off the front porch and ruined them. It used to be the custom to make baskets of flowers for your friends and leave them by the front door, ring the doorbell and run away on the first day of May.

We lived at the Desert Hotel in Coeur D'Alene once. We had one room. My mother slept on a cot and my brother and I slept on the bed. Our bathroom was in the hall and was shared with other guests. We would eat at the restaurant where my Mom worked, the Silver grille, where she was head waitress. We had wind up portable phonographs that we would play in the evenings. We had many records we enjoyed, such as one called Horses Horses Horses, that we would play while Al jumped on the bed. After school we would go to the restaurant to eat and then go to the room and wait for Mom to come at 8 o'clock. We were to be in bed when she got home, which we were.

The Royal Lineage

Mom rented a new two room stucco house on 4th street and we went to Roosevelt School. There was a front room, a bathroom and a kitchen. The front room contained a bed that dropped down from the wall, a cot and a dresser. Once I almost got caught in the bed while I was making it. I used to wash socks in the bathroom, but the rest of the clothes went to the laundry.

I used to do the cooking. I made a roast one time that pleased my Mom. I made a white cake with white frosting with walnuts on it. A family down the alley had a baby with a wicker buggy and I used to wheel the baby around to show off. My first experience with a radio was about this time when visiting Aunt Ida. They had a crystal set with earphones. Al, I, Uncle Lorence and Aunt Ida would sit and listen to shows like Amos and Andy and Ma Perkins.

We lived in the Antler Apartments downtown Coeur D Alene above two bakeries. There was a big kitchen, a living room and a bedroom. I cooked on a coal oil stove. The stove burned oil instead of gas or wood and it had burners that were lighted. I remember cooking link sausages on it.

We stayed at Aunt Midge and Berts, who worked at the same restaurant with Mom, for a while when I was in about the fourth grade. She wasn't really my Aunt, but we called her that. They had an older son, Del, a daughter, Hazel, and Bertie (Alberta May Rice), who was about six. They had a canary that was always flying around. They made their own home brew and had bottles of it around the house. Hazel used to sneak in and wear my mother's clothes, and even my underwear! My Mom was a flapper, with short hair and short skirts. She went out after work once in a while and she had a lot of friends.

The Royal Lineage

Mom got sick then, and went to the hospital and I went to stay with Aunt Emma, just behind Aunt Midge, and Al went to Aunt Fay's. We went to stay at Grandpa Stone's house after mom was out of the hospital. While she was recovering she did some housework for him. He was widower. He had just returned from a trip and had brought back some shells and a shark jaw. This was a larger house and Mom and I had our own room. I got St. Vitis Dance (a nervous disorder). I was having trouble controlling my arms and went to the doctor, who gave me medication. I went to stay at Aunt Ida's to recuperate. Mom found a job at the Silver Grille in downtown Spokane and lived in a hotel on Washington. I used to go visit her at the hotel. This was at the same time they were building the Paulson Building. Al was staying at Aunt Fay's at this time. He liked to chum around with her son Billy. Mom then went to stay with the Wilsons, some friends. Through them she met Harry Roskam, who she later married in 1930, when I was twelve years old.

Mom and Harry rented a house in West Spokane, a two story house with three bedrooms. Al and I each had our own bedroom, I attended Wittier School, fifth grade. The railroad ran right beside the house. We would stand outside and wave at the cooks on the train when it went by. The kitchen had a wood stove, electric lights, a kitchen cooler for refrigeration,and an indoor bathroom. Clothes were still washed by hand on a washboard with bar soap, rinsed in several tubs of water, wrung by hand and hung on a line to dry. We didn't care much for Harry right off,because we weren't used to having someone telling us what to do. Harry didn't know much about raising kids. Mom gave him most of her attention. Mom started doing more housekeeping at this time. Harry worked at Armor's Packing House slaughtering cows.

The Royal Lineage

Adam, Harry's dad, lived up the street from us. He and his second wife used to drop in for dinner once ¡n a while. Adam would eat and his wife would always say she wasn't hungry but would always say how good the potatoes were and eat a plate of potatoes. Later Harry's dad separated from his second wife and he came to live with us. Adam had a feather bed that he shared with Al. Later he moved on.

Harry got laid off work and went to work at a dairy farm just outside the city limits and we went to live in a furnished house at the dairy. I went to Windsor school and was in the fifth grade. This was a two room school house, with four classes in each room. The fifth, sixth, seventh and eighth grade was in my room. It was quite a walk to school. Once a seventh grade boy offered to carry my books home but I was too embarrassed. There was a big stove in the back corner and the kids had to help keep it clean. There was a big open water bucket near the entry door for our water. There were two doors to get into the school house, one for the boys and one for the girls. There were chemical toilets in the restrooms. Recess was outside.

I moved to Diamond Lake when I was in the seventh grade and went to school at Newport. We first lived with my Grandma and Grandpa Shively. Then we moved into Southwell's house, a boyscout camp worker. We stayed there for the winter. To get drinking water we had to walk a ways along the lake to the pump. There was a tramway to haul water up from the lake to wash clothes and take baths. We had an old cookstove. There was an outhouse. This was during the depression. We raised chickens and fished through the ice. That Christmas we decorated the tree with popcorn and a chain of colored paper. We covered walnut shells with cigarette package foil and we

The Royal Lineage

made stars out of cardboard and covered them with foil also. We got a large slab of bacon from Spokane from Uncle Pete. We went to Grandma Shively's and got gifts of a pencil tablet and pencil from Aunt Pearl and Uncle Charlie and a handmade hankie holder and an autograph book from Aunt Ida and Uncle Loren.

On my fourteenth birthday, in February, mother made me a birthday cake out of bread dough. My aunt gave me a pin for my hair. That winter I fell in the lake. Harry and Charlie were cutting wood across the lake. Mom, Harry, Al and I were walking across the frozen lake with a sled we were pulling. I was carrying our lunch in my arms. Harry cautioned us to watch out for the fish holes, but I stepped in one with my next step. The hole was covered with snow so I couldn't see them. I was wet up to my waist. Mother pulled me out (I always kid her about trying to save her lunch). We finished crossing the lake and Harry built a big bonfire to dry my clothes. Then we went home. Later I caught what I thought was a cold and on March 11, I left school early to see Dr.Slaughter. He said I had a heart problem. He used a fluoroscope that showed enlargement of the heart and a leaky valve. He gave me some medication and told me to go home and go to bed. I was sleeping on mattress made of shavings, containing chunks of wood. Aunt Fay was worried about me so she talked to her family doctor, Dr Hall, in Spokane. He drove 42 miles up to see me and gave me a prescription, that contained Styrchnine. A friend took the prescription to Spokane to get it filled. I was also not to eat raw apples, so he brought me some oranges.

Harry then got a job in Spokane working on building sewers. He moved us to a house on Olympic Ave. Uncle Case came and got me in his car, made me a bed in the back of the car, and drove me

The Royal Lineage

to his house until the family was settled into the new house. Al stayed in Newport to finish school, living with Aunt Minnie and Uncle Earl. I slept in the front room by the window on a single bed. They would carry me in and out of the house to the hammock in the front yard. I was not allowed to get up due to my heart problem. Al joined us after school was out. Lots of people brought me flowers, and kids came around me to play so I could watch. On July 4th was the first time I stood up and I had to learn to walk all over again. I had been in bed for four months. I was feeling better and the doctor said I could start being active again

We moved a few blocks away to Wellesley in an old shoemaker house. It had an outhouse, but had running water and still used washtubs for baths. That fall I started J.J. Browne school in the seventh grade. I spent recess lying down in the teacher's lounge. During the school year we moved to Mission and Ash, a lwo story two bedroom house and attended Bryant School. I still was very weak and not completely cured, and Dr. Hall advised me to quit school. I was just ready to start the eighth grade, but I never returned to school after that.

For fun we would play cards, take walks in the park and on the high bridge railroad tressle. My girlfriend Grace and her two brothers Billy and Clark, my boyfriend, would go to Natatorium Park, an amusement park with rides and a picnic area. My favorite ride was the roller coaster and the train and Fun in the Dark. They had a big fountain and a carousel that is now in downtown Spokane at the Riverfront Park. Clark was my boyfriend for over a year. He played the banjo and his brother played the guitar and we would sing. He moved away after a while. I rested at home for a while and took odd jobs babysitting two little boys that lived across the street. Then we moved to Broadway and Chestnut, a big house with an entry hall, parlor with a fireplace, dining room, living room. The kitchen was small with a wood stove. There was a full bathroom with tub. Everyone had their own bedroom. The roof had ornate structures on it. As I got stronger, I helped a friend with housework. Later I worked with Shoenberg's doing the housework, cooking and ironing. They had three girls I babysat. The baby was Doris.

When I was 18 I worked at the National Youth Association (NYA) cutting out dresses and made $9.00 a month. Through a mutual friend I met Gene. Her son, Eddie, had a band in a tavern in Spokane, that had a dancehall upstairs. Gene was a friend of her son's. I went with her to the tavern and there I met Gene. He took me dancing upstairs. He walked me home and told me how he was going to inherit money when he turned 21. He was 17 at the time. I asked him if he was related to the Stone's in Coeur d' Alene. He found out I knew all of his relatives better than he did. He had been living with his dad in California. We started going to dances and shows, and whoever could afford it paid. The popular dances of the time were waltz, foxtrot and two step. He worked at the NYA also, and went to barber college.

He proposed under a streetlight on the way home from the dance one night. We married March 3, 1937 in Davenport WA by the justice of the peace. His grandfather Feldhausen was a witness. He was 18 at the time, which required parental permission. Our first home was in an apartment with his mother, Jean. I was soon pregnant with my first son, Gene. I was sick all the time. In June, at six months pregnant, I took a bus by myself to Denver to visit my Dad, whom I hadn't seen in years. Dad only sent enough money for me to make the trip. He had remarried

The Royal Lineage

and now had six kids, four boys and two girls. They lived in a big house. He was a furrier at Denver Dry Goods.

I stayed two months with him and his wife, Mary. I was getting close to time to deliver the baby so I went to stay at the Salvation Army home and worked for my room and board. I didn't think I could make the bus trip back to Spokane in that condition. When I went into labor, they had a place to deliver babies and their doctors handled the delivery. Gene was born August 11, 1938, one month early, and weighed 5 pounds 5 ounces and was kept in an incubator. He was born with a cleft palate and couldn't be nursed. They used a special bottle to feed him. He also had yellow jaundice. We stayed at the home for six weeks and then they operated on his hare lip. Now he weighed 6 lbs and 1/2 oz at this time. Later they operated on his palate. I worked nights taking care of all the babies and patients. After Gene recovered, about six months later, we returned to Spokane on the train. Gene's mom was a proud grandmother and Gene was very proud of his son, showing him off whenever he could.

Gene worked at the hospital helping the nurses and doctors, and also as a caddy at the golf course and whatever odd jobs he could. We got a bigger apartment with two bedrooms, so we each had our own room. There were cockroaches in the kitchen and bedbugs in the beds. This was an old funeral home with high ceilings. It was heated with a little wood stove with a tall stove pipe to the ceiling. Once the stove pipe fell down and made quite a mess.

We later moved to another apartment in the same building with a wood cookstove I used to bake in. I did all the cooking and housework. Jean worked cleaning doctors' offices in the Paulson building. Rent was $16 per month, which we split. I became

The Royal Lineage

pregnant again with Johnny. My mother gave a baby shower for me at her house on 4th avenue. Most of the ladies were from Gene's side of the family. I got many nice things.

My water broke and Gene drove me in his mother's car to Deaconess Hospital, a few blocks away. I was there longer than expected because of problems with the afterbirth.

Johnny was born July 19, 1940. I usually washed clothes in the washing machine at the apartment and line dried them on a line with a pulley. When I was able, I went to mother's house to do my washing in her machine. I hung the clothes on a clothesline in her backyard. Once, I was carrying Johnny down the apartment stairs when I slipped and fell down the stairs. I hit my foot on a post at the bottom of the stairs and injured my foot, but Johnny wasn't hurt because I held him in my arms. This was on my way to mothers to do my laundry. Gene and Gene Jr were waiting for me in the car.

Once when I was nursing Johnny, the plaster from the ceiling fell and landed just where I had been sitting and nursing him. I had just gotten up and was lucky to not have been there when it came down.

When Johnny was nine months old, we moved to McCloud CA. Gene got a job in the sawmill working in the box factory where his father and cousins and uncle worked. We had a Buick sedan with the back cut off to make a pickup. We piled all our belongings into this car, and the two babies and drove.

It took three days to make this trip since the car lights would not work properly and we could only drive in daylight hours. Once we ran off the road accidentally and a passerby stopped and helped

The Royal Lineage

us get back on the road. We spent the first night at Biggs Junction in a cabin with two beds. I washed cloth diapers by hand and hung them to dry in the garage. The next day we drove to Green Valley where there was still snow on the ground. We stayed in cabins that had just been opened up for the summer and the stove was newly painted. When we heated it up, the smell was terrible. The next day we made it to McCloud. As we drove to the back of Gene's dad's (Gene) house, the axle on the car broke. We were so lucky we made it before this happened.

We stayed at Gene Sr's and Hilda's house until payday and we then found a house in Mt.Shasta. Gene and Gene Sr made a bed for Gene Jr and a chest of drawers for us, which I still have in my bedroom. This house had a small kitchen with a stove, sink and cupboards. We had an open window with a box sticking out, and running water from the roof to keep things cool.

There was a living room which had our eating table, high chair and chest of drawers along with a larger chair. The bathroom had a shower and toilet. We had a small radio given to us by my mother, which was our entertainment. Mom and Harry had bought this to listen to the world series when I was about 15 years old. I did the laundry on a washboard, with two big washtubs. I hung the clothes on a pulley line behind the house.

Then I discovered I was pregnant with Joan. The doctor in Mt. Shasta told me I have a heart problem and I needed an operation. I consulted the doctor in McCloud and he said everything would be okay. We moved to a duplex next to Gene's cousins, Bertie and Carl Hammond. They had a son,Carl, who was called Corkie, about the same age as Gene.

The Royal Lineage

Joan was born in the hospital in McCloud. The trip to McCloud was 10 to 15 miles and when I went into labor, it was a snowstorm and we almost got stuck. We drove to Gene Sr. house to drop off Johnny and Gene and went to the hospital, and as we entered the hospital, the nurse met us with the usual questions. The doctor entered and hollered down the hall to get me into the delivery room. Gene lit a cigarette and before it was half through, Joan was born, December 28, 1941.

Mother had come to visit from Spokane to stay with Johnny and Gene while I was in the hospital. They gave me a surprise shower at Bertie's house. Since Harry called and wanted her to come home, she left a couple of days before Christmas. Gene was really mad, since we had paid her way down. On Christmas day, I cooked a turkey. Bertie and Carl tried to go out to eat but nothing was open. We had them come to eat with us. Bertie didn't even help with the dishes, and I had to clean everything up in my very pregnant condition.